D0070664

CRUISIN'

Karts

By Lorraine Jolian Cazin

PUBLISHED BY
Capstone Press
Mankato, Minnesota USA

CIP
LIBRARY OF CONGRESS CATALOGING IN PUBLICATION DATA

Cazin, Lorraine Jolian.
    Karts/ by Lorraine Jolian Cazin.
        p. cm. — (Cruisin')
    Summary: Describes the small racer known as a kart, and the hobby/sport now of international proportions.

    ISBN 1-56065-072-9:
    1. Karting—United States—Juvenile literature. 2. Karts (Midget cars)—Juvenile literature. [1. Karting. 2. Karts (Midget cars)]
    I. Title. II. Title: Carts. III. Series.
    GV1029.5.C39   1989
    796.7'6—dc20   89-27915
                                      CIP
                                      AC

Photo Credits:
John Robinette

Capstone Press
P.O. Box 669, Mankato, MN, U.S.A. 56002-0669

CONTENTS

THRILLS AND CHILLS

Whether they drive them or watch them darting around the track at breakneck speed, karts fascinate people. Their ear-splitting noise and hyperaction provide thrills and chills. Which karter will take the lead in the race? Which karter will win the trophy? Karting was meant to be fun. Fun for the driver. Fun for the spectator.

Karts are the smallest of racers. They usually have no protective bodywork. The open racing car is designed to seat one person. The driver sits only a few inches above the ground. A basic kart has a 2-cycle engine and a bucket seat set into a tubular and springless **chassis.** The kart has tiny wheels. Some karts are equipped with twin engines. Others operate on **4-cycle engines.** Karts can lap most race tracks faster than a motorcycle with the same engine.

A karter is a person who drives a kart. Girls and boys as young as 8 years old can compete in races. Most events, however, require a karter to be 12-16 years old. Adults, as well as children, can be karters. One 75-year-old man is still driving in karting competition.

Karting not only is a sport, but a hobby. Anyone who owns a kart does not have to enter it in a race. They can take their kart to a track and, during "open practice," drive around the track just for pleasure.

IN THE BEGINNING

Little did Art Ingels realize, in 1956, that an invention of his would create a whole new industry. Little did he realize the use of his creation would result in a new hobby, as well as a new sport for people of all ages. And never did he think that the sport would go national—or international! When Art decided to build a "little car," all he intended to do was to have fun.

Ingels was working in Los Angeles, California, for the Kurtis Kraft Factory. The factory built the chassis for many types of Indianapolis race cars. Many days during their lunch hour, Art and his fellow employees would take the chassis of a quarter-midget car (miniature version of a race car) around the parking lot.

One day, Art noticed that there was a large amount of salvage tubing in some of the corners of the factory. At the same time, he heard there were thousands of surplus two-stroke West Bend single-cylinder engines for sale at a bargain price. The reason these engines were priced so cheaply was that the McCulloch lawn mower they had been made for had been discontinued.

Just for fun, Art decided to put together a car of his own. He attached one of the lawn mower engines to a steel tube frame. The engine was mounted behind the driver's seat. He added four wheels. He adapted a **chain** to connect the engine and the rear wheels. He fitted the car with pedals. He put in a steering wheel. He added

other necessary parts to complete the vehicle. When finished, the car weighed just over 100 pounds. For fuel, he used a mix of oil and gas, like the fuel used in a two-cycle lawn mower. It helped that Art was a mechanic so he knew what parts would be needed to make his car run. It helped that he knew where to put the parts. But most of all it helped that he had been designing, building, and driving hot rods for years.

At first, Art drove his little car only in the parking lot of the company where he worked. Then, after he had worked more on improving the car, he took it to the supermarket where he did his weekly grocery shopping. He asked permission of the owner to use the parking lot for racing his little car.

Racing in the "lie-down" style karts

The car went slowly. But it was exciting when he sped around the parking lot. Art felt like he was traveling at a much higher rate of speed then he actually was. This was because the car had no body and no windshield. And he was sitting so close to the ground. He was going 30 miles per hour—but it felt to him like he was going 100 miles per hour!

Art realized that people were willing to pay for cars like his. He believed these little cars would sell—especially in California. Art tried to get his boss, Frank Kurtis, to turn them out. But Mr. Kurtis said, "I'm too busy turning out race cars for Indy jobs."

Ingels and his friend, Lou Borelli, began to design and build some in their garages. The men built them for fun. Soon more and more people wanted to buy their cars, so they started a business. They called their cars "carettas," and sold them for $150.

At the same time, one of Art's friends also started making the little cars. From his muffler shop in Los Angeles, Duffy Livingstone began to sell and make his little cars with his partners, Bill Rowles and Roy Desbrow. Soon the three men were spending all their time building the little cars.

Soon other people decided to build their own cars. They used engines from chain saws and lawn mowers. They used chains from bicycles. They used wheels from hand trucks and wheelbarrows.

When Art Ingels first created his car he referred to it as the "little car." Some people called it a little cart. Then one day, Lynn Wineland, an advertising man and friend of Duffy and his partners, decided the vehicle needed a real name. He used the term "Go Kart." In 1957, the word "kart" was first used in auto magazines. After that, the sport was referred to both as go-karting and as karting. Today, the "go" has been almost entirely dropped. Recently, the term "Racing Karts" has been gaining acceptance. It is part of a movement to make karting a more serious form of motor sports competition.

Trailers are used for transporting karts to and from the tracks.

Loading a kart after a race

Sprint kart

KINDS OF KARTS

All karts have something in common. With a few exceptions, they lack any formal suspension system. Their wheels are tiny. They have no gearbox. With their low center of gravity, karts are easy to handle and control—even when they are speeding over 100 miles per hour.

Sprint Karts

A sprint kart resembles the original Ingels kart. One can identify it because of its "sit-up" driver's position. This position is designed for greater control on the twisty sprint courses.

Most sprint karts use either a single-**cylinder** 6.1 cubic inch or an 8.5 cubic inch air-cooled, two-stroke engine especially made for karting. The engines are mounted at the side rather than behind the seat. The fuel tank is located in front under the steering wheel.

Sprint tires are **slicks,** without **treads.** They are 2 or 3 times wider than the familiar treaded tires. This type of tire sticks to the asphalt track better. Sprint karts can cost $1,500 - $3,500.

Sprint racing is the oldest type of kart racing. It combines high speed and short distances. On a good track, some karts can **accelerate** up to 85 mph on the

straightaways. Most go 40-70 miles per hour. Sprint karts race on asphalt tracks that are 1/2 mile or less in length. Some tracks are asphalt ovals. Races include 3 separate short races called **heats.** A heat is usually 10 laps around the track. The final winner is the driver who has the highest total points from the 3 combined heats.

Road Racing Karts

Road Racing Karts are often referred to as enduro karts. They are called enduro because this type of racing is an endurance race. It is scheduled for running one hour! Enduro karts differ from sprint karts in that the driver is in a reclining position. He looks like a luge driver in the Olympics! Karters reduce wind resistance on their chests and abdominal areas by driving their machines in this "lie-down" position. The enduro has superior **aerodynamics.** It has only one gear. Most enduros use the same type of engine as the sprint karts use. Some have single engines and others have larger or dual engines. These can power the kart to go as high as 130 miles per hour! Most enduro karts travel 85-125 miles per hour.

The kart has large fuel tanks saddled on both sides of the kart. The tanks are larger in order to hold enough fuel for the long distances the kart will travel in the race. The kart has an exhaust system which may be adjusted while the kart is in motion.

Enduros run on full-sized, paved, road racing tracks used for sports car and Indy car racing. Some famous tracks used are the Indianapolis Raceway Park, Daytona, Portland International Raceway, Sears Point, Laguna Seca Raceway, Pocono, Riverside, Willow Springs Raceway, and Seattle International Raceway. Officials measure the length of the road race by time. The winner is the driver covering the greatest distance in one hour. Enduro racing is popular in England and France.

Enduro karts can cost $4,000 - $6,000. Because this is a more exacting and dangerous form of racing, both of the kart racing organizations recommend previous experience in sprint racing before an applicant receives an enduro license.

Enduro kart

Enduro kart

Speedway Karts

Dirt Karts have "sit-up" style driving. Their tires are wider and have treads cut in them to give better traction in the dirt. It is cheaper to do this sort of racing because tires last longer on dirt than on pavement. The engines have an air filter to prevent the engine from choking from the dust. The karts have a front fairing, which is a fiberglass panel that fits over the steering wheel. It serves as a shield to protect the karter against stones that might be thrown up from the track or other karters.

Racing action

Dirt racing is the most thrilling of all sprint classes. It all began when people wanted to race their karts but couldn't find the necessary asphalt tracks. Instead, they decided to use tracks that were built for stock car racing. The racing is done on an oval dirt track. Races are run on a 1/5 mile or less track. Sometimes races are held on small fairground tracks during county fairs. Like a sprint race, the competition has 3 separate heats.

Dirt karts can go 70 miles per hour. Most go 40-65 miles per hour. These karts are exciting to watch **broad-sailing** through turns. To broadsail, the driver pitches the kart sideways and slides through the turn with foot on the throttle. At Daytona, 500 to 600 karters participate in a speedway event. At one time, 50 karters may be on the track. Imagine them broadsailing! Isn't it good that there are rules for these karters? Can't you imagine the traffic jam if they didn't? Dirt karts can cost $1500 -$3500.

Karter ready to push into starting area

Superkarts

Superkarting arrived from Europe in 1979. Superkarts have been described as "expensive flying lawn chairs with clutches." The karts resemble the big cars racing at the Indianapolis 500. Acceleration and braking of superkarts is astonishing.

Drivers use a driving position that is between the sit-up style and the lie-down style. Using this position, the karter views the track while looking out over his feet. Bodies of the drivers are not enclosed as they are in the more elaborate karts called Formula Karts Experimental, which also include transmissions. Cockpits feature only a **tachometer** on the wheel. Some karts have their engines located alongside the drivers for more even weight distribution. This also makes it easier for the karter to fine-tune his vehicle during racing. The kart has a six-speed transmission, which is engaged through a pedal-operated clutch and a hand-operated gearshift. Superkarts reach speeds of 165 miles per hour. Most race at 130-160 miles per hour. Superkarts can cost $10,000-$15,000. Recently interest in this type of car has declined, because of its high cost and maintenance, and because of lack of available tracks.

HOW TO BEGIN

Years ago a boy or girl could build a kart from scratch. They could use tricycle wheels, left over 2 x 8s, some steel rods, washers, or other odds and ends to make a homemade one.

Today karts or complete kart kits with engines can be purchased. They may be bought at kart shops or ordered factory direct. People can put together any sort of vehicle that suits them. Sometimes a new production appeals to others and starts a trend. To

Working on a kart

enter a kart in competition, you must make it meet particular specifications. Used karts may be found through friends, or newspaper and karting magazine ads. Kart shops might be able to help you meet someone who is moving up to a faster class and would sell you their current model.

Once a kart is purchased, the main expense is engine rebuilds and new tires. Tires have an important job to do because they tie the vehicle to the ground. The more competitive a karter becomes, the more the cost goes up. Entering races means a kart will need more tires. The engine will need more rebuilding.

The pit area at a kart track

Where Do I Drive a Kart?

Years ago, karts were driven in alleys, on sidewalks, on school playgrounds, or on Main Street. Today, that is illegal. Karters must take their karts to specially designed tracks for karting. To locate a track, call a company listed under "Karts" in the yellow pages of the telephone book. Or write to the International Kart Federation (IKF) or the World Karting Association (WKA). These organizations have information about tracks and karting events. If a karter plans to compete, membership in one or both of these organizations is required.

A karter on the race track showing jacket, helmet, and gloves and a neck brace collar

What to Wear When Karting

It is important to wear clothing that will help protect while racing or driving a kart. A jacket and helmet is needed even during a practice session. Jackets and full-length pants should be of heavy-weight vinyl, nylon, or leather. A new nylon-duck fabric called "Cordura 1000" is now being widely used. There are also one-piece karting uniforms. Speedway suits feature elbow and knee padding and covered zippers. Some suits have a layer of aluminized, heat-resistant material on the sleeve. This prevents scorching an arm while adjusting the carburetor on the kart during a race. These outfits give the body protection if the kart overturns or if the karter is thrown off the vehicle.

A karter in a speedway suit, helmet, and gloves, pushes his kart into the starting area of the track.

When purchasing a helmet, look inside it for a sticker with the name "Snell 90." This indicates the helmet was upgraded in 1990 and has passed the Snell Foundation standards. The Snell Foundation tests and approves protective headgear for riders of bicycles and motorcycles, and for equestrians and car racers. Some helmets have a flip-down face shield or a bubble shield. Helmets protect the face and eyes from stones and rubber that is thrown from other karts while going around the track. Driving gloves are important to protect knuckles in case of an accident. Most karters wear high-top gym shoes. A great number of racers wear full-leather boots. Many karters invest in ear plugs to protect their hearing.

What Tools Are Needed

Working on a kart requires a kart stand. It is even possible to buy a motorized kart lift. Karts must have a starter. A hand-held one similar to the type used at Indianapolis is used to start the engine from a nut

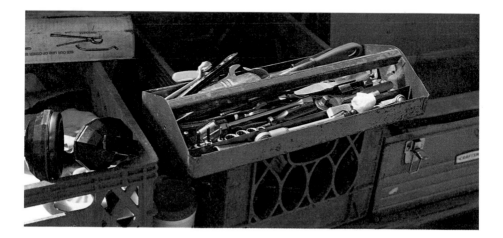

located on the clutch side of the engine. It is connected to a storage battery and not carried on board the kart. Because it is disconnected when the engine starts, someone other than the driver must operate it.

A toolbox is handy for the collection of tools needed to fit all the nuts and bolts on the kart. Karters need a chain lube, a gas can for the gas-oil mixture to run the engine, a drip pan, and a selection of spark plugs. Also, it is good to have a tire pump and tire pressure gauge. Most important, each racer must have a fire extinguisher.

A toolbox ready for use by the karter

SAFETY

Kart racing has a safety record better than any other form of motor racing. Accidents can happen and do happen in karting. There are not many because of the emphasis on safety from the two national karting organizations. Karters know they must observe safety rules. They know karts must be in good condition. Karts undergo a pre-race technical inspection. Before a kart even goes out on the track, it is checked for faulty

A meeting before the race to explain rules and give race information to the karters

construction and defective equipment that might endanger the safety of the karter or other karters. An emergency vehicle or ambulance with a stretcher is required during all events. Also required is a physician, paramedic, or qualified attendant and a first aid kit.

Tracks must have protective barriers along the raceway. This prevents spectators from being struck by a runaway kart.

The helmet or racing suit of a driver must show name, blood type, Rh factor, and any allergy or other important information in the event medical help is needed.

Race in progress on a track with protective barriers in background

COMPETITION AND CLASSES

A driver must be a member of either the International Kart Federation (IKF) or World Karting Association (WKA) in order to participate in events sponsored by these organizations. The IKF operates primarily west and the WKA primarily east of the Mississippi River. Sometimes their boundaries overlap. Both groups have similar regulations and rules for local, state, regional and national racing events. You can contact the organizations at the following addresses:

International Kart Fed.
4650 Arrow Hwy Ste B-4
Montclair, CA 91763
714/625-5497

World Karting Assoc.
PO Box 294
Harrisburg, NC 28075
704/455-1606

Kart and driver being weighed to determine class weight

The kart frame, not the driver, is the official entry in a karting event. Class structures are determined by age, driver/kart weight, and engine size and type. Class weight is determined by combined weight of both the kart and driver after competition. Types of engines are used to determine some competition **classes.** There are other classes which place no restriction on the type of engine used. IKF has over 65 different classes, 18 of which are for road racing alone!

Classes

Competition racing requires that the driver be 8 years old. There are various classes to enter in 2-cycle and 4-cycle sprint and speedway events. At the age of 16, drivers are eligible for adult events. A driver must participate and receive a finish position in 3 sanctioned events in order to receive a qualified road racing license.

The Pit

At each event, entrants are assigned an off-track pit area where driver and crew (usually 2 helpers) can do necessary work on the kart before the race. The driver may pull the kart there for emergency repairs.

The pit area during a race

Practice

Karters must demonstrate their driving ability to the satisfaction of the race officials during a mandatory practice period before being allowed to compete. All rules and procedures for competition apply to practice sessions.

Pre-Race Technical Inspection

The pre-race technical inspection takes place at an assigned impound area. Officials have many items to look over carefully before the race begins. They check

Karters leaving the pit area

the kart design for competition. The kart must be clean, and its tires should be new or in good condition. The wheels must have no defects. Fuel lines are checked to make sure they are safety wrapped at all connections. Brakes are inspected to make certain they are operating properly. The throttle is checked to be sure it closes automatically upon release.

Flags

Flags are the only way for karters and officials to communicate during the race. It is important that drivers memorize what each color stands for.

Green - Race has started.

White - One lap left in race. (sprint racing only)

White with Red Cross - Emergency vehicle on the track.

Blue - You are being overtaken by a faster karter. Make room.

Yellow - Caution, hazard on track. No passing. Slow down.

Yellow and Red - Waved together - Restart. Stop at start-finish line.

Red - Stop at once. Track unsafe. Go to impound area.

Black - used to signal particular drivers. A waved black flag tells a driver to continue one more lap at a slow speed and then stop by the racing official who is giving the signal. Usually means a kart has a mechanical problem such as a fuel or oil leak, or some other regulation is being violated.

Rolled Black Flag - warns driver that his driving technique borders on disqualification. If karter continues in the same manner, the kart will be black-flagged and possibly disqualified.

Black and Orange Ball - used for mechanical malfunction. Stop immediately.

Checkered and Black Flags - waved together - Finish is under protest. Used to end competition if suspicion of rough or illegal driving or unsportsmanlike conduct is present.

Checkered - End of race. Drivers are expected to continue around the track one more time at a reduced speed, then stop in the impounding area for post-race inspection.

Post-Race Technical Inspection

After each competition, karts and drivers proceed directly to the designated impound area. Kart and driver are weighed together. Class weight, kart size, legality of engine, exhaust system and silencer, fuel and tires are all checked out. Drivers may not add any ballasts (weights) to themselves or to their karts between the finish of the competition and weigh in. Winners are not announced until the inspection is completed. Inspections are thorough and careful. Karting rules are enforced. As a result, karting has an excellent safety record.

Awards

The IKF gives out the Duffy Award, the highest award obtainable in U.S. karting. It is named after Duffy Livingstone, a karting pioneer. To be eligible, a karter must participate in three separate IKF Sanctioned Racing Events since the previous year's Road Race Grandnationals. The races must not be run all in one weekend. Karters accumulate points to determine their starting position at the Grandnationals. Duffys are awarded in various classes for Sprint or Road Races. The karter who comes in first in each event is the winner of a Duffy Award.

PROFESSIONAL KARTING

There is an impressive list of champion-class auto racers who started out in karting. Emerson Fittipaldi, winner of the 1989 Indy 500, is one. Besides Fittipaldi, Nelson Piquet, Jody Scheckter, Ricky Rudd, Kevin Cogan, Scott Pruett, and Ayrton Senna used karting as a first step in a driving career. Two men who came from racing families, Michael Andretti and Al Unser, Jr., were teenage karters. Al went from karts to the Indy in only six years! Other karting graduates who became famous are Mario Andretti, Lake Speed, and Joe Ruttman.

Starting a kart using a starting motor and battery

In 1974, the first professional karting race was held. It was organized by experienced karters, Lake Speed and Lynn Haddock. They decided that a pro class would separate the drivers who karted daily from the karters who raced their karts as a weekend hobby. Those who race for money join an organization called the Professional Kart Association (PKA). This professional class has developed its own set of rules called the Expert Class.

Using a pull cord to start the kart

THE FUTURE

In the beginning days of karting, those five men—Art Ingels, Duffy Livingstone, Bill Rowles, Roy Desbrow, and Lou Borelli—intended for karting to be fun. Now, it still is fun. Kart racing just keeps growing and changing. But the future of this hobby and sport will largely be determined by the boys and girls who take the time to learn about karts, karters, and karting.

Karting is not only a healthy outdoor sport, but an easy way to learn driving skills. It teaches concentration, sportsmanship, and respect for the other driver's ability. Karters gain first-hand knowledge about car parts and how to repair engines. By asking questions, listening, observing, and reading, karters can keep up-to-date on this spectacular motor sport.

Ready to go!

The race is on!

GLOSSARY

Accelerate: To gain speed.

Aerodynamics: Force of air on a moving object.

Broadsailing: Dirt track technique in which kart is thrown sideways to slow its forward motion enough to make a turn.

Chain: Device transmitting engine power from crankshaft to rear axle by linking clutch and axle sprockets.

Chassis: Frame of car.

Classes: Groups of cars that run at about the same speed with similar engines and body styles.

Cylinder: Chamber in internal combustion engine through which piston moves when driven by the combustion process.

4-cycle, four-stroke engine: Internal combustion engine that performs intake, compression, power, and exhaust with four strokes of the piston.

Heat Race: The first competition for the day. Usually 10 laps.

Slicks: Smooth tires used only on dry circuits.

Straightaway: Straight section of a track.

Tachometer: Instrument measuring engine's revolutions per minute. Used to adjust clutches and check output of engine.

Tread: Pattern cut into tires. Used in wet weather. Grooves allow water to escape.

2-cycle engine: Engine which produces a power stroke for each crankshaft revolution.

INDEX